This book is dedicated to all who find Nature not an adversary to conquer and destroy, but a storehouse of infinite knowledge and experience linking man to all things past and present. They know conserving the natural environment is essential to our future well-being.

ROCKY MOUNTAIN

THE STORY BEHIND THE SCENERY®

by Michael T. Smithson

Michael Smithson, a graduate of Evergreen State College with a B.S. in wildlife biology, also completed additional work in museum studies at the University of Colorado. During his 15 years as a career professional with the National Park Service, Michael served 9 years as a naturalist at Rocky Mountain National Park.

Rocky Mountain National Park, *located in north central Colorado, established in 1915, preserves the massive grandeur, rich scenery, wildlife and wildflowers of the Rockies' Front Range.*

Front cover: Hallet Peak from Dream Lake, photo by Joe Arnold, Jr. Inside front cover: Colorado River headwaters, photo by Jeff Gnass. Page 1: Young pine, photo by Mike Donahue. Pages 2/3: Storm at sunrise over Bear Lake, photo by Tom Algire.

Edited by Mary Lu Moore. Book design by K. C. Dendooven.

Fourth Printing, 1993

*H*ealth and hope for all who enter here, and that once within the mellow-lighted and peaceful place, all would responsively hear the treetops whispering: "These are your fountains and gardens of life; kindly assist in keeping them."

—Enos Mills, 1924

The Rocky Mountains! Towering peaks and crystal lakes beckon all to this mountain wonderland. Elk graze quietly in valley bottoms surrounded by open parklands of ponderosa pine. Dense subalpine forests invite exploration and hide delicate orchids amid their green tangle. Higher still, on top of the world, alpine tundra mantles the peaks with a dazzling display of lilliputian wildflowers.

Soaring above a sea of plains and plateaus, the mountains provide relief from the intense heat of the lowlands. Over a century and a half ago, a member of the Long Expedition declared that the "whole range had a beautiful and sublime appearance to us, after having been so long confined to the dull uninteresting monotony of prairie country. . . ." How many visitors today share his thoughts!

Trail Ridge Road, the highest continuous paved highway in the nation, takes us to the heart of this special world. Rising to more than 12,000 feet into the sky, the road provides vistas of ancient rock and magnificent mountains. Deep glacier-carved canyons cut into the earth, providing depth and grandeur. Streams and falls fill the senses with bubbling music, their waters split by the Continental Divide. This is where the mighty Colorado River begins its 1,400-mile journey to the sea.

Here in the Rockies wildlife truly abounds. Bighorn sheep leap from rock to rock while cougar silently stalk them. Hundreds of species of birds grace the mountain slopes and fill the air with song.

Each year the peaks attract thousands of climbers. "Here the beholder may scale beyond the clouds far heavenward, and gaze upon a world at his feet!" Longs Peak, the highest mountain in the park, is climbed by the experienced and the novice, the young and the old, on well-worn trails and upon immense cliffs.

Take time to experience the special qualities of each season at Rocky. In autumn the forests are splashed with gold, and canyons echo with the bugling of elk. Winter's harshness assures the skier and the mountaineer a glimpse of frosted beauty, while a fleeting spring turns meadows from brown to verdant green. Look to the skies at night in any season, for the heavens are painted with brilliant stars.

The beauty, solitude, and wildness we encounter help us experience the splendor of this magical place—Rocky Mountain National Park.

DAVID MUENCH

The naked rock exposed in the mountain cliffs is a book that reveals the ancient history of the park. To understand this book we need to journey back—back nearly two billion years to when the oldest rocks in the park were created. We would need a boat, for the earth that would become Rocky Mountain National Park lay at the bottom of an ancient sea. Unknown lands and mountains

Trail Ridge view

Shaping the Rockies

surrounded the water; bacteria and primitive algae were the only living things.

As the forces of erosion took hold, the silts, sands, and clays were swept from distant lands. The sediment, like snowflakes from an immense storm, drifted slowly, silently, toward the bottom of the sea. Layer after layer accumulated over millions of years and mixed with lava flows until the deposit was tens of thousands of feet deep.

Imagine the pressure of this weight. The force was so great and the temperatures so high that the material began to change, or *metamorphose*, like a caterpillar changing into a butterfly. The sedimentary rocks, squeezed by massive weight from above, transformed into *gneiss* (pronounced "nice") and *schist*. These metamorphic rocks now

Nature's relentless forces sculpted Rocky's magnificent peaks and canyons. Layers of sedimentary rock from ancient seabeds once covered the entire region. As the mountain range pushed into the sky, these sedimentary layers eroded away, exposing a geologic puzzle of different rock types.

The twisted skeleton of a limber pine stands guard near an outcrop of metamorphic rock. Tremendous pressures squeezed and folded these rocks into fantastic patterns.

form the tops of the park's mountains. Gneiss, with its alternating bands of grey, white, and black minerals, looks like petrified marble cake. Schist is darker and more finely banded.

Although large veins of gold and silver were discovered in the Rockies, little has been found within the boundaries of the park. Shiny flakes of mica (MY·cah) in schist look like gold to youngsters, but have no economic value. This lack of mineral wealth was one of the main reasons why the park could be established.

Gneiss and schist aren't the only rocks in the park, however. Between 1.4 and 1.7 billion years ago the metamorphic rocks, still buried by sediment above, were attacked—invaded by red-hot molten rock from below. The magma forced its way into cracks and veins in the older rock and actually dissolved the gneiss and schist in places. Had it worked its way to the surface it would have flowed out as lava. But it was trapped deep in the earth, blanketed from above by thick insulating layers. It cooled slowly, over perhaps ten million years, into granite and pegmatite. This mass of igneous ("born of fire") rock was 30 miles wide and now forms the basement of the park's mountains.

Caught in a Vise

If you could have stood on the plains and watched the last 300 million years speed by, you would have found that the current mountains are not the only ones that have existed here. In fact, they are at least the third set. The others were stripped to the ground by erosion, as the mountains you see today will be. The forces that cause the earth to rise are just now being understood. The planet's crust, which is not as rigid as once thought, has been broken into huge moving plates that float on the hotter rock beneath it. Like an ancient demolition derby, these plates have rammed against each other for billions of years. As the North American Plate ripped apart from Europe and Africa it moved west—as fast as five inches a year—and slid over the plates of the Pacific Ocean floor. Great pressures squeezed the continent together, and the rocks of this region were caught as in a vise and crumpled into great folds, like the wrinkles and dimples of your face when you smile. Pieces of the Pacific plates extended far under North America, where they melted in the intense heat and caused the entire area to rise.

The ancestral Rockies were islands in a shallow sea, probably no more than a few thousand feet high. Amphibians, the first vertebrate animals to abandon the oceans, basked on their shorelines. The islands were gradually reduced to hills when sand dunes and then great fern-covered swamps surrounded them. Dinosaurs emerged from these swamps to dominate the land

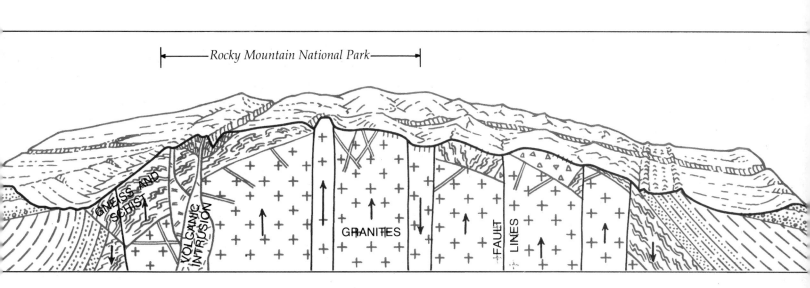

GNEISS AND SCHIST

VOLCANIC INTRUSION

GRANITES

FAULT LINES

for over 160 million years. Once again the seas invaded, completely covering the Rockies.

Forces within the earth could not be held back, and the current mountains rose from the sea about 75 million years ago. The sediments on their surface eroded away, exposing the ancient rocks: the gneisses, schists, and granites we see today. The mountains were raised and eroded to rolling hills one last time before a final upheaval lifted the entire region to its present elevation. The flat top of Longs Peak and the rolling uplands of Trail Ridge are thought to be remnants of these hills.

Around 37 million years ago distant volcanoes buried in ash all but the highest mountains. Molten rock later forced its way to the surface near the northwest corner of the park. Specimen Mountain, along the Continental Divide near Milner Pass, was once thought to be a volcano. But the volcanic rocks that cap it and nearby peaks are welded ashflows from volcanoes outside the park.

The pressures that caused the mountains to rise were great enough to break the rock into massive blocks that often moved independently of each other along cracks, or faults. Many blocks, like Longs Peak and the mountains along the divide, rose while others dropped, thus helping erosion form a number of the park's canyons. It is possible that the Estes Park basin was lowered more than a thousand feet. The up-and-down movements of these blocks helped create the striking scenery we see today.

THE DESTROYERS

The process of erosion, when combined with the vast span of geologic time, is incredibly powerful. What seems so permanent, so unmoving, is constantly changing. Even humans play a part. When you throw a rock into the river, you move

DAVID MUENCH

An odd mushroom-shaped rock looms near the Tundra Nature Trail off of Trail Ridge Road. This formation's light-colored granite erodes more quickly than its dark brown cap of schist. These rocks are more than a billion years older than the volcanic rock found in the Never Summer Range in the background.

"In the throne of the mountain gods." Sunrise lights the East Face of Longs Peak and Chasm Lake. At 14,255 feet, Longs is the highest mountain in northern Colorado. Vertical joints in the granite allowed water and ice to cleave the Diamond, a thousand-foot cliff. This rock wall is considered one of the classic alpine climbs in North America.

Water splashes, slides, and tumbles over Alberta Falls. Year after year it patiently wears away at the rock, pushing tiny grains of sand and pebbles ever closer toward the plains below.

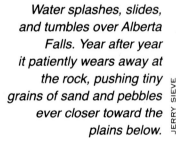

JERRY SIEVE

the rock a little closer to its destiny. Denver, Colorado, is built on the ashes and bones of the previous mountains—the *old* Rockies—that washed onto the plains. Some rocks from the park have been found as far east as Nebraska and Kansas. Fossils, records of the living past encased in sedimentary rock, were carried away from the mountains, leaving few clues about what lived here. The same sedimentary layers that once covered the Rockies still flank the mountain's east and west slopes. These fossil-bearing deposits reveal many secrets of the history of life on earth.

Water affects rock a number of ways. It sneaks into tiny cracks, then freezes, expands, and splits the rock apart. This process often occurs in the mountains, where temperatures dip below freezing at night and warm far above it during the day. Carbon dioxide from many sources, including our breath, mixes with rain to make a mild acid that dissolves the cement that holds rocks together.

Mechanical and chemical weathering break bedrock into boulders, boulders into rocks, rocks into pebbles, and pebbles into sand. Gravity tugs and pulls the material ever downward. Running water hurries the process. Nothing standing, either natural or man-made, is free from its power.

As the mountains rose, streams set to work

carving valleys into rolling land. The Continental Divide, the nation's backbone that divides the waters that flow into the Atlantic and Pacific oceans, was created. This ridge is not always the highest point of land, however. Visitors at the Alpine Visitor Center are often surprised when told they must drive westward four miles to a lower elevation to reach the divide in this region.

Wind is also an effective eroding agent in this area. Gusts have been measured at over 200 miles an hour—strong enough to blow a man away. Enos Mills, a prominent early nature guide, discovered this when he climbed Longs Peak in winds in excess of 175 miles an hour. As he neared the top of the mountain he made the ascent upside down. "There was no climbing, the wind sucked, dragged, pushed, and floated me ever upward." Visitors often ask why there are large, heavy logs on the roof of the Alpine Visitor Center. They are there to keep the roof on! The winds pick up every loose grain of sand and hurl it toward the plains below.

Gradually the rocks that covered the ancient granites and metamorphics were stripped away.

When the rock above it is removed, granite, which is formed under great pressure, expands, cracks, and peels in layers like the skin of an onion, creating *exfoliated* rocks. Lumpy Ridge is a good example of this process. When weathered, these rocks often look like gigantic "cow pies" left in the meadow by some mythical beast.

Even plants contribute to the unending erosion of the earth. We have all seen roots cracking the pavement in our cities. *Lichens* (LIKE·ens), small, ancient plants that grow on rocks, also produce carbonic acid that slowly dissolves the rock piece by piece.

ICE ON THE ROCKS

The mountains would still be high, rolling hills cut by river valleys, had it not been for the glaciers—massive rivers of ice that ripped and gouged the rock into magnificent peaks. When the great continental ice sheets reached into the northern United States, thousands of feet of snow fell in the mountains. In time, that snow turned to ice and gave birth to alpine glaciers. These moving

Hallet Peak and Flattop Mountain form one section of the Continental Divide. This ridge separates the continent's waters and forms a barrier for west- or east-bound storms.

Hurricane-force winds blast the ridges of the Divide during the winter. They create a truly arctic environment on the mountain summits.

KENT & DONNA DANNEN

Lumpy Ridge was once called "Thathaa-ai atah," or "Little Lumps," by the Arapaho Indians. Today, rock climbers share these weathered granite knobs with prairie falcons, turkey vultures, and bighorn sheep.

JOE ARNOLD, JR.

Golden light reflects off the still waters of Chasm Lake. Surrounded by thousand-foot cliffs on three sides, this beautiful lake fills the basin of a glacial cirque. Rock quarried by frost action and former glaciers accumulates in talus piles at the base of the vertical walls.

MIKE DONAHUE

tongues of ice were hundreds, even thousands, of feet thick. Most of these glaciers remained within the park's boundary.

Imagine standing near a glacier 100,000 years ago. A mammoth might be eating tundra flowers in a meadow nearby. The glacier is alive: cracking, creaking, and groaning as it creeps downward, pulverizing the earth beneath it. The ice is soft, about the same density as your fingernail, and by itself cannot do much to change the shape of the land. But it is full of rocks temporarily frozen and locked into place. Fashioned into a great file, the glacier uses the mountain's rocks to carve stream-cut valleys into U-shaped canyons.

It's easy to see the work of glaciers in Rocky Mountain National Park today. Bowl-like *cirques*

Reduced to a shadow of its former self, Taylor Glacier still presents a challenge to ice climbers. Glaciers ripped and pried rock from the mountainside and carved the scenery that made Rocky popular. Taylor is one of the park's five active glaciers. Much of the snow that feeds these small moving ice bodies is blown down from the ridge tops.

MIKE DONAHUE

The U-shaped Fall River Canyon was once filled with a river of ice at least a thousand feet deep.
This glacier also created Sheep Lakes, which have no natural outlets. As minerals accumulated in the mud
the ponds became natural salt licks for bighorn sheep.

formed at the head of each glacier when melt-water seeped into cracks in the rock, froze, and expanded. The ice acted like a crowbar, prying rocks from each headwall. The 1,200-foot vertical east face of Longs Peak was carved this way. In the Never Summer Range, where the rock is softer, the same action formed huge piles of rubble or *talus.* Some of these piles are still cemented together with ice and move down the mountain as rock glaciers. *Arêtes,* or ridges, were created between glaciers in different valleys. Given enough time, two glaciers would eat at the rock separating them until only a sharp, needlelike ridge remained. With their spires and towering walls, arêtes and cirques are a climber's paradise.

Glacial striations are lines scratched in the bedrock by stones held fast in the ice. They show the direction each glacier flowed. As the ice pushed down a valley, it quarried depressions where the bedrock was fractured and weak. The deeper basins filled with water when the glaciers

retreated, leaving chains of "beaded" lakes. Bear Lake, Dream Lake, and Emerald Lake are excellent examples. In fact, most of the lakes in the park originated from the work of glaciers.

The mass of earth and rock the glacier moved was eventually cast out along the edges and ends of the ice in *moraines*—great piles of rubble. The South Lateral Moraine along the Bear Lake Road is a classic example. When the glacier that filled Big Thompson Canyon retreated, its terminal, or end, moraine dammed the river and created a lake. Water later cut through the dam, drained the lake, and left the flat, open area we call Moraine Park. Horseshoe Park was also formed in this way.

Today's glaciers are tiny compared to the ones that once existed. Most of the mountain sculpting was done between 15,000 and 1.6 million years ago when the great glaciers surged forward again and again before they disappeared. The five current glaciers are probably remnants of a

Sharkstooth, Petit Grepon (little climb), and The Saber are three colorfully named spires on the arête (sharp ridge) above Sky Pond and the Lake of Glass.

Little Ice Age that began nearly 4,000 years ago. Although the west side of the park receives more snow than the east, and once had the largest glaciers, the "modern" glaciers are on the east side, where winds blow across the Continental Divide and pile the snow deeper. Some geologists wonder whether enough snow has fallen in recent years to keep the glaciers alive. If too little snow accumulates, a glacier will stop moving and die. The icefield will lie dormant until temperatures drop and snowfall increases.

For at least 2,000 years, treeline, the upper limit of timber growth, has been gradually lowering, which indicates that the climate in this area is cooling again. Many scientists believe we are in the middle of a temperate period and that the glaciers will come again one day. If they do, they will tear away at the rolling mountaintops, reducing them to jagged spires and horns, and will once again change the shape of the Rockies.

Although most ridge tops were blown free of snow during glacial times, the effect of ice was still felt. The ground was permanently frozen. It would thaw a little during summer, and moisture trapped in surface soils by the ice below turned the tundra into a marshy bog. The unstable earth slowly slid down the mountainside and slumped into ridges called *solifluction terraces*. Many are no

longer active, but they can easily be seen from Trail Ridge Road.

Trail Ridge also has excellent examples of patterned ground. When moist earth freezes and thaws, rocks within are pushed about and literally squeezed out of the earth. If the land is nearly level, the rocks sort into polygons; on steeper slopes they form rock streams, stripes, and garlands. Some rocks are heaved halfway out of the ground, making strange natural "tombstones" for unknown spirits.

Most earth-shaping processes take hundreds of lifetimes to affect the land, although a few can be surprisingly quick. Avalanches are fairly common during the winter, and one avalanche chute in Fall River Canyon has been dubbed Old Faithful by park rangers. Its habit of destroying a section of Fall River Road has frustrated park superintendents for decades.

At the base of the canyon in Endovalley another geologic event occurred on July 15, 1982. A little after 6:00 A.M. a worker heard a deafening roar that at first sounded like a plane crash. He soon realized the sound was caused by millions of gallons of water rushing down Roaring River and guessed that Lawn Lake Dam had given way. Trees in the water's path were uprooted, and car-sized boulders were tossed about like pebbles. Five miles below the dam, Endovalley Road was buried under 44 feet of sand and rock as the torrent slowed and spread, forming what geologists call an *alluvial fan*. The largest boulder the water moved weighed 452 tons. This area, with its huge piles of rock and uprooted trees, is an excellent example of the power of water.

Whatever forces have been at work, the faces of the mountains will continue to change. Our image of their permanence is a myth we hold onto during our brief glimpse of their evolution.

SUGGESTED READING

CHRONIC, HALKA. *Time, Rocks and the Rockies.* Missoula, Montana: Mountain Press Publishing Company, 1984.

HARRIS, ANN, and ESTHER TUTTLE. *Geology of National Parks.* 3rd ed. Dubuque, Iowa: Kendall Hunt Publishing, 1983.

RICHMOND, GERALD M. *Raising the Roof of the Rockies.* Estes Park, Colorado: Rocky Mountain Nature Association, 1974.

In the shadow of the Spearhead, retreating glaciers dropped their load of rock—great carving tools left by departed ice giants.

Geologists believe the flat top of Longs Peak and the gentle rolling mountaintops of the Front Range are erosional remnants of an ancient rolling plain.

Life in the Mountains

The mountains, with all their splendor, would be desolate without the thin mantle of life that blankets them. It is this profusion of living things that attracts us most. We are excited by the sight of a deer slipping through the forest and enchanted with the delicate beauty of a mountain wildflower. The variety of plant and animal life here is often surprising. A number of different habitats are hidden between the canyon bottoms and the ridgetops: ball cactus blooms in one spot, arctic gentian in another.

If you drive from Denver to the Arctic Circle, you travel through many different climates and habitats. You can take this same trip in a few hours by driving to the top of Trail Ridge Road. In the mountains the different life zones are stacked atop each other like a layer cake.

Gravity is one of the elements responsible for this remarkable diversity; it holds the molecules of air close to the earth. The top of Longs Peak, nearly three miles high, pokes through this thin veil. Air here is almost half as thin as

LARRY BURTON

Three different life zones rise above Moraine Park. Annual precipitation on top of the peaks is two to three times greater than it is in the meadow below, and the temperature difference on any given day can be 25 degrees. Plants and animals have adapted to these diverse climates.

Trail Ridge Road winds across the "land above the trees." This alpine tundra is similar to the vast arctic regions of Alaska and northern Canada. In Colorado over 300 species of specially adapted plants grow in these mountaintop meadows.

A bull American elk, or wapiti, enjoys a moment's rest.

*New life can indeed spring from disaster.
This lake formed in 1982 when boulders and
debris from the Lawn Lake Flood
dammed the Fall River.*

*Bistort's white blossoms wave above
a riot of tundra wildflowers.*

it is at sea level. Not only does this make it hard to breathe, but the thinner air also loses heat faster. In fact, the air is 3 to 5 degrees (Fahrenheit) cooler for every thousand feet you climb in elevation. The Alpine Visitor Center at 11,796 feet is almost always 20 to 35 degrees colder than the plains of Denver. The types of plant communities that grow in the park and the animals that live in them are largely governed by this temperature gradient.

The MONTANE LIFE ECOSYSTEM, with its open ponderosa pine forests and grassy meadows, covers the lower elevations of the park. The SUBALPINE ECOSYSTEM—similar to the vast boreal forests of northern Canada—is higher; and the ALPINE TUNDRA carpets the tops of the peaks.

Mountain ridges facing south receive more sun than their north-facing counterparts: snows melt more quickly, less moisture is available, and temperatures are warmer. At lower elevations the north side of a ridge may support a thick Douglas-fir forest, while pine, sagebrush, and even cactus grow on the south side. This variation in exposure further subdivides the patchwork of plant and animal communities.

Water also alters the distribution of life. The mountains are a barricade to storms approaching from both sides of the park, and as moisture-laden clouds are pushed up the mountainside, temperatures drop and snow or rain falls. The tundra receives two to three times as much snow as do the lower-altitude towns of Estes Park and Grand Lake. Most of this snow is later blown into the subalpine ecosystem.

Many of the winter storms come from the west, causing most of the snow to fall on that side of the park. It is often referred to as the "wetter, better side," while the eastern slopes bask in the "banana belt." In spring, however, storms approaching the east side from the Gulf of Mexico create "upslope" conditions in which many feet of wet, heavy snow can fall in a short time, adding much-needed moisture.

Like its geology, Rocky Mountain's climate is a dynamic, changing process. The life it supports has changed hundreds of times throughout mil-

Colorado blue columbine, the state flower of Colorado, is fairly common in moist areas. Once endangered by flower pickers, it now thrives in protected areas such as the park.

Beaver ponds provide refuge and water for many animals. Beaver are mainly active at night, but can sometimes be seen near dusk.

lions of centuries. Ancient sand dunes, swamps, and glaciers attest to earlier fluctuations. We can only guess what will come next.

Rivers, Lakes, and Ponds

The mantle of snow covering the Rockies in winter is the lifeblood of these mountains. As it melts, little creeks tumble down the hillside to become engorged and swollen rivers. This seasonal change is surprising—and dangerous—to unsuspecting visitors who are not aware of the

Cacti are found at lower elevations on the drier east side of the mountains. Defensive spines discourage animals from tasting the succulent stems.

19

power of mountain streams. The American dipper, or water ouzel, braves the current to search for small aquatic insects. This small drab-gray bird bobs from rock to rock along the streamside before it disappears under the water, only to emerge seconds later with its beak full of larvae.

Colorado River and greenback cutthroat, the native trout that lived here, nearly disappeared in the early 1900s because of overfishing and watershed damage. Their biggest threat, however, came from exotic (introduced into this area) rainbow, brook, brown, and Yellowstone cutthroat trout. These fish, which were easier to rear in hatcheries, outcompeted or hybridized with the natives until the indigenous trout were nearly eliminated. At one time the greenbacks were even considered extinct. Fortunately a few isolated populations were later discovered and are now used in a restocking program to bring back Rocky's "original" fish. The effort has been so successful that their status was lowered from the endangered- to the threatened-species list.

Water is not the only element that flows in the valley bottoms. Cold air from above has surprised more than one unprepared camper as it follows rivers downward at night. Temperatures here can be substantially lower, and growing seasons shorter, than a higher area 100 feet away. In this envi-

Hidden Valley Creek supports an amazing diversity of life. Mayfly, stonefly, and caddisfly larvae cling tenaciously to the rocks along the streambed. Greenback, cutthroat and brook trout can also be found in this creek's waters. Greenbacks were once endangered, but an active restocking program has helped reestablish them.

A pair of mallards paddle near shoreline. Throughout the summer their newly hatched chicks can be seen tagging behind the female. Mallards are the most common ducks in the park, but many other species of water birds may be found in the small lakes and ponds.

ronment the beautiful Colorado blue spruce grows at lower elevations. Yet not all blue spruce are blue. The color is a waxlike coating found only on the needles of certain individuals and on newer growth.

The only snake that is common in the park is also found near streams. This small nonpoisonous reptile is the wandering garter snake. Although its bite won't puncture your skin if you pick it up, it will deposit a smelly substance on your hand, a repellant to predators and curious children.

Most streams eventually tumble into one of the park's 150 or more mountain lakes. They are *very* cold; only the brave or foolish attempt to swim or wade in them, and then only for a short while. The colder temperatures and shorter growing seasons of the higher lakes exclude all but the hardiest of flora and fauna. This absence of living things makes the water so clear that the bottom of a lake appears only an arm's reach away. Life is still present, even in the smallest of tundra pools. Throughout the short summer, fairy shrimp, mosquito larvae, and other insects dart from one side to another.

Despite frigid temperatures, the lower lakes support a surprising amount of life. Bear Lake alone contains about two tons of minute plants and animals known as *plankton*. Tiny freshwater clams, snails, sponges, and a host of invertebrates thrive at lower elevations. Tiger salamanders, often referred to as a fish with four legs,

Legend has it that Abner Sprague, one of the area's first settlers, planted this magnificent Colorado blue spruce when he developed a resort near here in the early 1900s. Squirrels sometimes use the tree's stiff branches to dry their harvested mushrooms.

An American dipper pauses below its nest full of hungry young. This nondescript bird walks underwater along stream bottoms in search of food. Formerly known as the water ouzel, the dipper usually builds its nest near splashing cascades or falls. Ouzel Falls and Ouzel Lake were named after this interesting fellow.

A beaver pushes an aspen branch toward the bottom of his pond, where he will lodge it in the mud along with other branches. Underwater brush piles form the beaver's sole food supply when ponds are frozen over during the winter.

are occasionally seen swimming alongside trout. Leeches—the non-blood-sucking variety—act as the lake's sanitary engineers.

The beaver is the largest animal found in park waters. Their ponds provide the beaver with protection from most enemies and support large numbers of birds and other wildlife. The muskrat is often mistaken for the beaver, but it is easy to tell them apart by their tail; the muskrat's is thin and ratlike, whereas the beaver's is large and flat. Moose are rarely seen, but their num-

bers are growing in the Kawuneeche Valley; they were introduced near the northwest corner of the park in 1978.

One of the most dangerous creatures in the park also lives here. *Giardia lamblia,* a microscopic protozoan, is found in most waters, especially in beaver ponds and lower streams. Unwary visitors who drink water without properly treating it may find their vacation cut short by abdominal cramps and diarrhea. Fortunately, this "beaver fever" is easily treated at the doctor's office.

Beaver ponds have altered Hidden Valley's landscape for hundreds of years.

The Meadows

. . . The rocky island in the meadow gave a bird's-eye view of the drama unfolding below. Shrill warning whistles pierced the dawn as the coyote stalked, hoping to surprise an unwary ground squirrel. He suddenly sprang high into the air and dove head first at his prey. The rodent was gone in three bites—and the hunter continued his patrol.

Mountain meadows, or parks, have attracted animals and people for thousands of years. Their open spaces were easy to hunt in, farm, and homestead; they provided good grazing for live-stock and wildlife alike. The term "park" is sometimes confusing. In Colorado many of the mountain grasslands are called parks and are often named after the first family who settled there. Estes Park and Allenspark are good examples; these towns are not associated with national or state parks.

Some of these meadows are successional, which means that the grasses will in time be succeeded by trees from the surrounding forest. But there are also many meadows that are climax, or permanent. Grasses in Moraine and Horseshoe

Overleaf: The Front Range stretches across the horizon above Sprague Lake.
Photo by Joe Arnold, Jr.

Bighorn rams fight grueling battles each fall to determine breeding rights. The clash of their horns can be heard over a mile away. Thousands of bighorn sheep once roamed this area, but they were nearly eliminated in the late 1800s. Effective park management has increased their numbers in the park.

parks grow better than trees do in the fine glacial soils of these ancient lake bottoms.

In Moraine Park a tree-covered knob of rock protrudes from the meadow. The rocky knob was probably an island when the glacial lake existed thousands of years ago. Trees grow easily in its thin, rocky soil. Cattle once grazed nearby on exotic grasses planted by ranchers. These grasses, and the weeds associated with them, still persist. Many of the animals living in the meadow use them for food.

The Richardson's ground squirrel, or "picket pin," is common. Its habit of standing up straight reminded early settlers of the groundstakes to which they tied their horses. Above ground, the squirrel is prey for the coyote, fox, and red-tailed hawk. Below, it is hunted by the longtail and shorttail weasels, which are thin enough to follow the squirrel down into its burrow. The badger uses its keen sense of smell and long claws to dig up this rodent. The hunting area looks like it has been bombed. Dirt is strewn about, and the land is peppered with large holes.

As the day draws to a close and dusk settles over the land, the wild song of the coyote fills the air. The high-pitched yips and yaps were once described as a "howl which the animal let out, ran after, and bit into small pieces." A lonely chorus strikes a forgotten chord deep inside, a reminder of wilderness and of a more rustic way of life. The coyote eats whatever it can catch, usually rabbits and rodents, but it is also a scav-

Incorrigible beggars, the golden-mantled ground squirrel and three kinds of chipmunks can be found wherever people congregate. Chipmunks are smaller, quicker, and have striped faces.

enger. Winter-killed elk and deer provide a large portion of its diet in this season. The number of coyotes probably increased to fill the gap left when wolves and grizzly bear were eliminated from the region by settlers.

Bison once shared the meadows and tundra with the elk, but an occasional skull is all that reminds us of their presence. There was seemingly no end to the game when settlers first arrived in this area. This abundance led to commercial-market hunting to feed the mining camps and the growing town of Denver. One hunter recalled that he "made contracts for a minimum weekly supply of three tons of assorted big-game meat . . . I was to get 10 cents a pound for elk, deer, and antelope, 12½ cents for mountain sheep, and 15 cents for bear." By 1877 very few elk were seen east of the Continental Divide. Most of the thousands in the park today are not native; they descended from the few surviving west-side animals and 28 elk transplanted from Yellowstone National Park in the early 1900s. They've done well since then—too well in fact.

In summer many elk move to the tundra and subalpine forests, where food is abundant. You can spot them near treeline along Trail Ridge Road at dawn and dusk. Early winter snows force most of them to lower elevations and into ever-dwindling wintering areas. The Park Service acquired and removed many of the private ranches and lodges within Rocky Mountain's boundaries, but commercial development of grasslands outside the park has continued at an in-

creasing pace. Park management is working with other agencies to develop solutions to this complex problem.

The meadows of Horseshoe Park are also a good place to see bighorn sheep—the symbol of Rocky Mountain National Park and of the State of Colorado. The sheep work their way down from the higher mountains, not so much to eat the grass, as the mud. The soil around Sheep Lakes in Horseshoe Park has high concentrations of salt, iron, and other essential minerals for these animals.

Bighorn sheep are sometimes confused with mountain goats (there are no mountain goats in the park), and they can readily be distinguished from deer and elk by their "longjohns"—large white rump-patches that extend down the back of their legs. Specimen Mountain, near Milner Pass, is also an excellent place to see sheep but is closed at the higher elevations to protect lambing areas.

We sometimes see more than we expect when we observe wildlife, however.

. . . The sheep were grazing quietly near the highway when the coyote approached. People were astonished to see the herd scatter, then rush wildly across the road—leaving a lamb behind. The predator quickly took advantage of the situation. Everyone witnessed the natural process of life and death that has existed for millions of years. They quietly watched the coyote struggle to pull the carcass across the meadow to its den of waiting pups.

Long tufts of hair on the ears of Abert's squirrels give them a rabbitlike appearance. This hair is shed every year.

Mountain bluebirds provide an extra splash of color. Their early arrival is a sure sign that spring is just around the corner.

A battle of another kind takes place in the trees near the meadow, but on a much slower scale. The roots of the ponderosa pine cover almost as much area below ground as does the visible part above. They can extend as far as 100 feet out from and 40 feet below a single tree. In their fight for water, roots from different trees often meet underground and suck the earth dry. This intense competition creates the open parkland associated with these trees, making them a delight to walk through and camp under.

Some of the older trees give off a sweet, vanilla-like scent. Their long needles, as John Muir wrote, "give forth the finest music to the winds." Vacationers have long associated the ponderosa with dry climate and temperatures that are "just right." The tassel-eared gray or black Abert's squirrel also likes these trees and feeds almost exclusively on the pine's seeds and twigs.

Mule deer browse on the nearby squaw currant, sagebrush, and bitterbrush. Mountain bluebirds use these shrubs for hunting perches; the intense blue of the male brightens the landscape. This environment is also the home of the Rocky Mountain wood tick. An open south-facing slope, such as the one Moraine Park Campground is built on, is an ideal tick habitat. Found mainly in the spring and early summer, this spiderlike bloodsucker, once attached, can transmit Colorado tick fever and a number of other diseases. Frequent checks of skin and clothing are recommended in tick season, as a tick usually crawls around a few hours before attaching.

On the north side of a ridge, where temperatures may be ten degrees cooler, ponderosa are replaced by Douglas-fir. Man's interference with natural fire led to overcrowding in these forests. Such overcrowding caused the forests to become weak and more susceptible to insect attack. Spruce budworm larvae eat fir and spruce needles; if they destroy enough foliage over the years, the trees die. In an effort to bring the ecosystems back into balance, park management is reestablishing fire in undeveloped areas. Charred stumps and tree scars prove that fire has been present in nearly all park forests at one time or another.

When fire does sweep through an area, the apparent destruction is short-lived, for aspen or

A red-naped sapsucker presents to his mate a mouthful of ants gleaned from nearby trees. This woodpecker was once called the yellow-bellied sapsucker.

lodgepole forests quickly invade. These two trees are the Jekyll and Hyde of the mountains. Aspen groves burst with life and color, while lodgepole stands seem to be biological deserts.

Lodgepole is also called fire pine, as its cones release most of their seeds only when temperatures reach 110 degrees or more. This allows the tree to recolonize burned areas quickly. Their long, straight trunks made good teepee poles and lodge materials for Indians and settlers.

Precious little light gets through the lodgepole's dense canopy to the few plants growing on the forest floor, but the silence is occasionally shattered by falling pine cones and the scolding of a chickaree, or pine squirrel. It might appear that the squirrel is intentionally throwing a cone at an intruder, but it is more likely that the creature is harvesting food. Many chickarees have a taste for mushrooms, including those poisonous to man, and carry them into the trees for drying.

In moist areas a light forest fire with lower temperatures may stimulate the growth of quaking aspen instead of lodgepole. The leaves of these beautiful white-barked trees shimmer in the slightest breeze. French trappers told the legend that the Cross on Mount Calvary was made of aspen, and that to this day the trees tremble with shame. Actually, the flattened leaf stalk allows the leaf to move back and forth, exposing both sides to sunlight.

Beneath the trees, dazzling wildflowers of all shades and colors, such as golden banner, daisies, and larkspur, speckle the ground. There can be no finer way of enjoying a sunny Rocky Mountain morning than lying on your back in a grove and gazing into the vibrant sea of green and blue.

Warbling vireos sing from delicate nests suspended from aspen branches, while a hollow tapping indicates a woodpecker is nearby. The heartwood of aspen is often rotten, making it easy to drill nest cavities. Once abandoned, these woodpecker homes are later used by bluebirds, swallows, wrens, and squirrels, among others. Sapsuckers drill small lines of holes in the bark of aspen and conifers to eat not only the sap but also the insects that are later attracted to it.

The battle-scarred trunks of aspen reveal that elk, beaver, and other mammals eat the nutritious but bitter green tissue under the bark. Once this cambium layer is girdled through, the tree dies. In successional groves the aspen are eventually replaced by other trees, but at lower elevations the more permanent stands of aspen are suffering. Overpopulations of elk can kill entire groves that have existed for hundreds of years.

ERWIN & PEGGY BAUER

One of the fastest birds in the world stands guard over its kill. Peregrine falcons were once fairly common throughout the West, but the use of persistent pesticides such as DDT nearly forced them into extinction.

Aspen groves, like this one in Horseshoe Park, are home for many species of birds.

JERRY SIEVE

Higher up the mountainside reigns the dark emerald-green beauty of the subalpine forest. Sharp spires of Engelmann spruce and subalpine fir reach into the sky, while moss, orchids, and blueberry bushes carpet the forest floor. Shafts of sunlight pierce the dense canopy, highlighting a tangle of fallen logs and the young trees they nurture. The trees' branches shed snow easily, and for good reason: the deepest snows accumulate here. Depths of five feet or more provide water for the thirsty lands and cities far below.

The subalpine region is the black bear's haunt. Rarely seen, bear do "come out of the woodwork" every few years to rummage through backpackers' tents for food. This may be in response to a poor food year. Snowshoe hares, which change color from summer brown to winter white, hop through the forest on their large hind feet. Chickarees also live here, sharing the trees with raucous Clark's nutcrackers and gray jays. These camp

MIKE DONAHUE

Wildflowers and plant life are especially lush near creeks in subalpine meadows.

JOHN GERLACK—DRK PHOTO

Clark's nutcrackers, named after William Clark of the Lewis and Clark expedition, cache thousands of conifer cone seeds for their winter and spring food supply.

Watch out for raucous Steller's jays when you are eating!

ERWIN & PEGGY BAUER

robbers have adapted to an unending supply of peanuts and potato chips from humans. It's tempting to offer handouts, but artificial feeding harms both the animals and the ecosystem. Squirrels and chipmunks at scenic overlooks bite and also transmit disease. It is far better to view them from a distance as wild members of this mountain domain.

Northern goshawks also frequent the subalpine. This fierce hunter defends its territory with vengeance, and people are not excluded. Trails have been temporarily closed to prevent hawks from harrassing innocent hikers. One bird snatched a ranger's hat and carried it off some distance before letting it go!

KRUMMHOLZ—THE ELFIN FOREST

The forest's march up the mountain is abruptly halted by harsh extremes of weather. Between the elevations of 11,000 and 12,000 feet the sparse water, cold temperatures, and strong winds make the survival of trees impossible. At tree limit, or timberline, one finds *krummholz* ("crooked wood" in German). These miniature forests of spruce and fir create a knee-high world to explore; trees less than a foot high can be hundreds of years old! Winds laden with particles of sand and ice blast bark and prune unprotected growth. Branches grow on the downwind side, creating lopsided "banner trees," reminiscent of flags flying in the wind.

At timberline small islands of trees hide behind rocks and spread flat in depressions. Some of these islands actually migrate; their protected branches take root downwind and thrive as the exposed branches die.

White-tailed ptarmigan (TAR·mih·gan) can be spotted around willow shrubs at treeline. They turn white in winter and motley brown in summer—providing camouflage that needs to be seen to be believed. The feathered feet of these chicken-like birds provide insulated support on the snow.

Striking evidence of fires that burned near timberline over a hundred years ago still exists. Solitary gray spires above Rainbow Curve and on Jackstraw Mountain near Trail Ridge Road remind us that life grows and decays very slowly at this elevation. A lowering treeline makes it even harder for these trees to reestablish themselves.

KENT & DONNA DANNEN

Subalpine firs near treeline brace against the fierce winds of winter. These banner trees easily give away the predominant direction of the wind. Their branches grow only on the leeward side of the tree trunks.

NPS PHOTO

Treeline marks the victory of the arctic environment. Here the climate proves too harsh for trees to survive.

31

Although more subtle than New England autumns, the tundra's display of color in late August and in September surprises many visitors. Many of the red hues come from the chemical anthocyanin, which helps the plants survive in freezing temperatures.

A dense community of cushion plants hug the ground. The alpine sandwort's white flowers are less than ¼ inch wide.

ALPINE TUNDRA—ON TOP OF THE WORLD

Beyond the trees extends a land few have the pleasure of experiencing: the alpine tundra. This windswept area is similar to the vast treeless expanses of Alaska, Canada, and Siberia. It is easy to remember that temperature decreases with altitude up here, for sweaters, rather than shirtsleeves, are the rule. On a typical summer day it can be hailing one minute, snowing the next, and sunny and calm the rest of the afternoon.

Along Trail Ridge Road you can throw snowballs even in August. The pink snowbanks found this time of year are caused by communities of algae. This "watermelon snow" smells and tastes like the real thing, but don't be tempted! It concentrates airborne radioactive elements and acts as a laxative.

Much of the snow that falls here in winter is blown away by winds well in excess of 100 miles an hour. Thirty-foot drifts are created in places, while ground is exposed elsewhere. As little as two inches of precipitation reaches the soil in these barren areas, creating an alpine desert. Too little or too much moisture, combined with intense ultraviolet radiation and a six- to eight-week growing season, creates conditions that only the hardiest of plants can survive. About 25 percent of the species growing here are found on the arctic tundra as well.

The most obvious adaptation to this severe climate is plant height. Tundra flowers are referred to as "belly plants" because you need to lie on your belly to get a good view of them. At three feet above ground winds are blustery, but temperatures are warmer and winds much calmer at three inches.

Many of the plants in the tundra contain anthocyanin, a chemical "antifreeze" that turns sunlight into heat. Tiny hairs also prevent heat and moisture from escaping and act as a sunscreen. The woolly alpine sunflower, or Rydbergia, is appropriately named "the old man of the mountain."

All the plants at this altitude are extremely susceptible to people's carelessness. A piece of litter or the scuff of a boot can injure a 50-year-old plant. Many feet can trample a community that will take centuries to regrow. To prevent damage, hardened trails have been provided in heavily used areas along the road. In other locations visitors can spread out and, wherever possible, walk lightly from rock to rock.

NPS PHOTO BY FRANK SMITH

Snowbanks harbor thriving communities of microscopic organisms in late summer. The pinkish tinge is caused by algae which also contain the chemical anthocyanin.

Elk, like many people, come to the high country during summer to beat the heat and escape insects. Cow elk have been known to give birth to their calves on snowbanks! Elk herds are usually seen near treeline at dawn and dusk.

In their frantic search for food, busy pikas seldom stop long enough to be photographed.

TOM & PAT LEESON

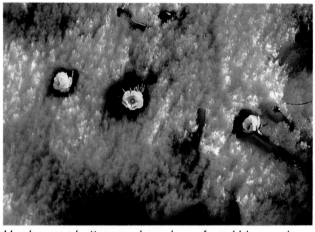

Hardy snow buttercups have been found blossoming many inches under the snow.

KENT & DONNA DANNEN

JOE ARNOLD, JR.

What better way to enjoy a bright sunny day? Yellow-bellied marmots frequent rock outcrops on the tundra, but need to keep a wary eye for coyotes, foxes, badgers, and eagles.

C. W. SCHWARTZ—ANIMALS ANIMALS

Secretive northern pocket gophers are rarely seen above the ground. Their extensive tunnel systems allow them to feed on plant roots and tubers.

Hikers enjoy a moment's rest high in Glacier Gorge. Many tundra pools have large underlying blocks of ice, or permafrost. If the ice melts in late summer, the waters vanish into the soil.

A number of mammals inhabit this fragile land. Yellow-bellied marmots, relatives of the woodchuck, bask lazily on sun-warmed rocks. They seem to do nothing but eat, sleep, and sunbathe all day long. In contrast, pikas (PIE·kas), members of the rabbit family, endlessly scurry about, gathering harvested plants into miniature hay piles.

The most influential animal in this ecosystem, the northern pocket gopher, is rarely seen. Found at all elevations in Rocky Mountain National Park, the gopher lives underground, eating roots and tubers of plants. Its habit of digging yields enormous amounts of earth that bury plants. One biologist estimated that an active group of gophers moves more than four *tons* of dirt in a year. But this seemingly destructive activity is an important part of the soil-building process.

Weasels and coyotes hunt the smaller tundra animals, and bands of elk and bighorn sometimes roam the area. Eagles, falcons, and ravens rule the sky during the short summer, but most fly to balmier climates as fall turns to winter. The autumn colors of the tundra are beautiful in their own right; their shades of scarlet and bronze paint the mountaintops.

The autumn season is fleeting, however. Heavy snows begin falling near the end of September, and 30-foot snowpoles must be placed so that the road can be found next spring. Temperatures plunge. Trail Ridge becomes increasingly difficult to keep open. Drifts accumulate on the road faster than plows can clear them. When the gates are finally closed for the year, the arctic world is left behind in the eternal silence and fury of winter.

OTHER SEASONS

In the meadows below, splashes of golden aspen color the mountain slopes. Autumn is still in full swing. The eerie bugling of a bull elk echoes across the valley, warning all that he alone is master of his harem. A challenger locks antlers, and they bully each other through the crisp grass. Later in the season mature bighorn rams challenge each other in a remarkable display of strength. The sounds of clashing horns are heard a mile away. Despite their possessive actions, rams sometimes discover that a younger male will run off with the female while they are fighting!

For most animals winter is a time of austere survival. Ice freezes the top of the ponds, confining beaver to their lodges and the icy waters below. Pikas continue their business in the coldest of weather while white ermine (summer's weasel) quietly stalk them. Ptarmigan scratch snow-caves in the soft snow. These homemade shelters give warmth and protection from the wind but are sometimes buried in storms. When skies clear, the birds pop their heads up through the snow.

Marmots and ground squirrels spend the winter in a state of suspended animation. These true hibernators sleep the winter away as their metabolism drops to an incredibly slow rate: their heart may beat only four times a minute. This seems like an easy survival strategy, but hiberna-

Winter snows pose no problem for the white-tailed ptarmigan. During storms these chickenlike birds roost in small snow caves, protected from the raging winds.

tion is one of the leading causes of death in these mammals. Fat reserves don't always last as long as winter does.

Aboveground, elk and sheep nuzzle snow aside to reach dried plants. Their thick coats trap warmth close to their bodies and also provide good hiding places for ticks and other parasites. Winter will take its toll, especially among the weak. But spring always returns to sustain those who survive.

Springtime, punctuated with heavy snowfalls, begins fitfully in the Rockies. But by May the dry grasses in the lower meadows are replaced with vibrant new growth. Life springs from every nook and cranny, greeting hibernating animals awaking from their long winter sleep. Wildflowers bloom first at lower elevations, then spread up the mountainside, bathing the Rockies in color. Once again the brief summer bursts forth.

A curious short-tailed weasel momentarily interrupts its hunt.

Golden aspen grace a hillside beneath Ypsilon Mountain.

SUGGESTED READING

ARMSTRONG, DAVID. *Rocky Mountain Mammals.* Estes Park, Colorado: Rocky Mountain Nature Association, 1975.

MARINOS, NICOS, and HELEN MARINOS. *Plants of the Alpine Tundra.* Estes Park, Colorado: Rocky Mountain National Park, 1981.

MUTEL, CORNELIA, and JOHN C. EMERICK. *From Grassland to Glacier.* Boulder, Colorado: Johnson Publishing Company, 1992 (reprint).

NELSON, RUTH A. *Plants of Rocky Mountain National Park.* Boulder: Colorado Associated Press, 1982.

TRIMBLE, STEPHEN. *Longs Peak: A Rocky Mountain Chronicle.* Denver, Colorado: Lahey Printing Company, 1984.

The *Tundra*

Like miniature soldiers on a bitter front, alpine plants have evolved many special adaptations that help them survive in the arctic environment. Harsh winter winds blast the tundra free of snow in some places and pile it 30 feet deep in others. These drifts may last into August and thus create an extremely short growing season for plants beneath the snow. The available moisture, wind exposure, soil conditions, and animal disturbances create a mosaic of alpine plant communities across the tundra.

American bistort, alpine avens, and western yellow paintbrush are just a few of the flowers flourishing in this mountainside flower garden. Many of these plants grow in temperatures just above freezing. If transplanted to lower elevations, they quickly die in the warmer climate.

Alpine sunflowers and whiproot clover brighten a rocky ledge above Forest Canyon. The sunflower's large yellow head takes several years to develop and blossom.

JOE ARNOLD, JR.

BUDD TITLOW

Skypilot graces alpine and subalpine meadows alike. At the lower elevations many of these plants exude a less-than-appealing odor that discourages raiding ants.

NPS PHOTO BY DONNA DANNEN

NPS PHOTO BY MICHAEL SMITHSON

Insects also must be well adapted to the colder climate. Bees' wing muscles perform poorly when temperatures dip below 50° F. Flies perform well at cooler temperatures and are responsible for pollinating many tundra flowers.

NPS PHOTO BY MICHAEL SMITHSON

NPS PHOTO BY MICHAEL SMITHSON

Plant hairs, such as the ones on the stem of this narcissus anenome, are found on many alpine plants. Ranging from whispy coats to wooly cloaks, these hairs reduce water loss, trap heat, and protect plants from intense ultraviolet radiation.

The abundant alpine avens is Rocky's "yellow rose of the tundra." Its fernlike leaves turn shades of magenta in fall.

Those Who Came Before . . .

The elk nervously glanced across the tundra in the direction of the thrashing sounds. They grazed less now—heads alert, anticipating unknown danger. The low stone wall guided their movements toward the hilltop, where men hidden in pits waited silently. As the spears struck their mark, the remaining animals panicked and scattered across the windswept knoll. Although the butchering tools were made from stone, their razor-sharp edges helped make the task easy; the meat would last until the next kill.

Different peoples and generations of hunters built game-drive walls and ambush pits. The broken spear points and scrapers left by these ancient nomads tell only a part of their story. Neither legends nor myths remain to help us envision what life might have been like thousands of years ago.

The Clovis and Folsom points of mammoth hunters indicate that humans ventured into the Rockies at least 11,000 years ago. At least 6,000 years ago cool subalpine meadows provided relief from two long periods of heat and drought known as the Altithermal. But tribes that came later used the area of Rocky Mountain National Park mostly for summer hunting.

Little more is known about human presence before the arrival of modern Native Americans. Ute Indians, for whom the state of Utah is named, held the mountains until the late 1700s, when the Arapaho Indians entered the region from the Great Plains. The Arapaho were only one of many tribes pushed westward by the expansion of Anglo-American civilization. Their search for plentiful game brought the Arapaho into conflict with the Utes, and the Continental Divide became their battleline. One Arapaho said, "In those days a man was always fighting. He was always moving around with very few possessions, camping in bad weather, and was likely to be wounded in some battle . . ."

Although the region of Rocky Mountain National Park was used mainly for summer hunting, the Indians left their mark upon the land. Teepee rings and other evidences of summer camps were found throughout the park when settlers first arrived. Large river boulders had been carried to the top of Oldman Mountain, where Native American religious ceremonies called vision quests were held. Now only mountain place names remind us of these banished tribes. "The places that knew them in their pride shall know them no more forever."

EXPLORERS AND SETTLERS

Claimed first by Spain, then France, the Rocky Mountains spawned tales of unknown wealth in their towering peaks. It was the lure of furs and gold that brought trappers and prospectors to the Rockies. American and French trappers probably explored the valleys of the Big Thompson

It has been rumored that small elves can sometimes be seen on park trails.

Longs Peak provides an inspiring background for Bear Lake

The rugged mountains of the divide were first viewed as barriers to westward movement by early pioneers. Only later did people's attention turn to scaling the peaks' lofty summits. Mount Powell, in the background, was named after John Wesley Powell, the first westerner to climb Longs Peak.

STUART SCHNEIDER

Rufus Sage, one of the few mountain men who wrote about his travels, provided in 1843 the first account of what was probably the park area: ". . . beautiful lateral valleys, intersected by meandering watercourses, ridged by lofty ledges of precipitous rock, and hemmed in upon the west by vast piles of mountains climbing beyond the clouds . . ." He went on to philosophize that one "might here hold daily converse with himself, Nature, and his God, far removed from the annoyance of man. . . ."

Sixteen years later Joel Estes and his son Milton discovered the same land while on a hunting trip. Milton later penned, "No words can describe our surprise, wonder and joy at beholding such an unexpected sight." They became the first family to settle in what is now Estes Park, surviving by raising cattle and shooting game for the market. Patsy Estes served "splendid meals of wild game, hot biscuits, and cream . . ." and swept the cabin's floor with the wings of eagles.

The Estes family spent less than six years in the mountain valley that is named after them. The winters had proved too harsh, so the land was traded for a yoke of oxen. However, the beauty of the area and the splendid mountains that surround it could not be kept secret for long. As more people came under the spell of the Rockies, homesteads began to dot the landscape.

Longs Peak towered silently above this new influx of people. At 14,255 feet, Longs is the tallest mountain in northern Colorado, and many have aspired to conquer it. Despite stories of Indians trapping eagles on its summit, the editor of *The Rocky Mountain News* declared that no creature had gained or would gain the top "unless it had wings to fly." In 1868 he proved himself wrong when he reached the summit with John Wesley Powell, who later explored the Grand Canyon. A member of the Long's Peak team threatened to leave one of Powell's heavy biscuits on top as an "everlasting memento."

In 1873 Anna Dickenson made the first recorded ascent by a woman. She was followed shortly thereafter by Isabella Bird, a somewhat stocky and out-of-condition Englishwoman, who was literally dragged up the mountain. Her guides related that by "alternately pulling and pushing her and stimulating her with snow soaked in Jamaica ginger, we got her to the top." She later chronicled her experiences and helped popularize the area in her book *A Lady's Life in the Rocky Mountains.*

The English Earl of Dunraven moved into the area in 1873 and attempted to buy Estes Park for

and Colorado rivers, but they left little evidence of their presence. The change of men's preference to hats of silk rather than of beaver quickly brought this colorful era to an end.

In 1820 the Long Expedition officially recorded the location of the park's highest mountains. Yet Major Stephen H. Long was never closer than 40 miles to the peak that bears his name. He later argued that the plains below were "extremely disagreeable" and "wholly unfit for cultivation." Time and water for irrigation have proved differently.

Revered first for its minerals, and then for its water, the Kawuneeche Valley held promise of quick wealth. Miners' claims proved barren though, compared to the mother lodes discovered south of the park. This valley contains the headwaters of the Colorado River. Originally known as the Grand River, the Colorado was renamed after an intense political battle.

his own use. By 1880 he claimed nearly 15,000 acres for his private hunting preserve. But many of his claims were fraudulent, and opposition to his scheme later forced him to sell much of the land for $1.25 an acre. Lord Dunraven did help popularize the area by commissioning the famous artist Alfred Bierstadt to create a painting of Longs Peak.

In the Kawuneeche Valley, on the western slope, claims of a different kind were made. The promise of gold, silver, and quick riches brought prospectors from near and far in the late 1870s. The boom towns of Lulu City, Gaskill, and Dutchtown sprang from the earth and attracted a motley assortment of humanity. One author characterized the inhabitants as "a curious lot—bearded miners, dirty laborers, strong-armed bull-wackers, thin-lipped gamblers, men of every character, and women of no character." Their dreams were shattered when the mines did not produce. The towns

vanished as quickly as they had appeared, and only grizzly bear remained to haunt their streets.

Water, rather than gold, became the real treasure of the Rocky Mountains. Farmers from the eastern plains knew the Western Slope received more moisture, and they made plans to transfer much of it to their side of the divide. One of the early large projects was the Grand Ditch, a 14-mile canal built near the ruins of mining camps in the Never Summer Mountains. The ditch intercepts snow-fed streams as they tumble toward the Pacific-bound Colorado River and diverts the water to an east-flowing river. Dams also raised the level of many existing lakes before the area was designated as a national park.

But water storage was not without its problems. When the 79-year-old Lawn Lake Dam burst in 1982, floodwaters caused damages of over $31 million.

Neither water nor precious minerals could be-

Native Americans and prospectors crossed these beautiful alpine meadows. It is easy to see why the mountains were later referred to as "America's Switzerland."

A tarn, or alpine lake, shimmers below Andrews Glacier. Although none of the park's glaciers are easily reached, those who complete the strenuous hikes necessary to arrive at them are well rewarded with breathtaking vistas.

JOE ARNOLD, JR.

NPS PHOTO BY BILL SONTAG

A park ranger–naturalist explores the tundra with a group of visitors. Throughout the summer months Trail Ridge Road makes this mountain world accessible to everyone.

The Diamond on Longs Peak poses a challenge for the most experienced climber. This grueling vertical wall usually requires two days to ascend.

MIKE DONAHUE

gin to match the attraction of the mountains' splendor. Word of "America's Switzerland" spread rapidly. Rocky was heralded as a land where "the sun never shone more brilliantly, the flowers never blossomed more beautifully, and the waters never chanted more hypnotic music . . ."

New wealth was to be made providing accommodations for the growing tourist trade. At least a dozen lodges, resorts, and dude ranches operated within the future boundaries of the park. Stead's Ranch in Moraine Park even boasted a golf course. In time the owners sold their property to the federal government, and the land was

JOE ARNOLD, JR.

Twin Sisters Peak floats like an island above a sea of foaming clouds. Views such as this have inspired mountaineers for over a hundred years. In 1922 Enos Mills wrote, "When one climbs a high pinnacle on the vast cathedrals of the world . . . all the glad hopes and dreams he may have had are his again, and all life is a tranquil dream."

restored to its natural condition. Along the Colorado River the Never Summer Ranch reminds us of this era. During the summer, visitors can imagine what life must have been like on an early dude ranch.

Just outside the park the Longs Peak Inn was operated by Enos Mills—climbing guide, naturalist, writer, lobbyist, storyteller, snow surveyor, miner, and cowboy. Enos tramped endlessly across the Rockies, braving storms, riding avalanches, and studying wildlife. He was one of the first to propose establishing a park in this region. Mills's original concept stretched from the Wyoming border south to Pike's Peak and would have protected a thousand square miles of mountain wilderness. But mining interests and political realities quickly cut his proposed area in half.

Mills solidified support for the controversial park by giving lectures across the nation and writing hundreds of letters and articles. His persistent efforts, combined with those of other conservationists, led President Woodrow Wilson to sign the park's enabling legislation on January 26, 1915. Heralded as the father of Rocky Mountain National Park, Mills's love, respect, and concern for the natural beauty of this land paved the way for our enjoyment today. At the park's dedication he proclaimed, "In years to come when I am asleep forever beneath the pines, thousands of families will find rest and hope in this park . . ."

Fall River Road, built with convict labor in the early 1900s, made the high peaks of the newly established park accessible to everyone. The road was so steep that Model T's had to drive up sections of it backward! The opening of Trail Ridge Road in 1933 created a safer, more scenic, route. Climbing to 12,183 feet, the alpine highway crosses and recrosses the Ute Trail—a path used by Indians and pioneers for centuries.

Today when we sit quietly in a meadow we might recall those who passed by here before: prehistoric hunters, Indian war parties, fur trappers, explorers, and settlers. Their tracks are gone, but their presence somehow remains, locked in distant memories of long-forgotten times.

SUGGESTED READING

ARPS, LOUISA WARD, and ELINOR EPPICH KINGERY. *High Country Names: Rocky Mountain National Park.* Estes Park, Colorado: Rocky Mountain Nature Association, 1977.

BIRD, ISABELLA L. *A Lady's Life in the Rocky Mountains.* [1879] Norman: University of Oklahoma Press, 1960.

BUCHHOLTZ, C. W. *Rocky Mountain National Park: A History.* Boulder: Colorado Associated University Press, 1983.

KAYE, GLEN. *Lulu City: Colorado River Trail.* Estes Park, Colorado: Rocky Mountain Nature Association, 1983.

SAGE, RUFUS B. *Rocky Mountain Life.* Lincoln: University of Nebraska Press, 1982. Originally published in 1846 as *Letters and Scenes in the Rocky Mountains.*

ROCKY MOUNTAIN
NATIONAL PARK

Nature's Heritage

Rocky Mountain National Park exists for us to enjoy—and protect. The thin mantle of life requires constant vigilance if it is to survive the impact of millions of people. Rocky usually receives the same number of visitors as Yellowstone National Park, but it is only one eighth the size of Yellowstone. Under this pressure the philosophy "take only pictures, leave only footprints" no longer suffices. If we can photograph wildlife from a distance, the animals remain undisturbed for the next visitor. In walking lightly we leave the pristine wilderness as we found it.

Still, there are difficult questions to be answered. Can there be too many people in the park at one time? Should private vehicles be restricted in heavily used areas? Should the wolf be reintroduced? How can the razor's edge between preservation and use be defined?

Like the ancient Rockies, this place of nature is rapidly becoming an island. Designated as an International Biosphere Reserve, Rocky serves as a source of comparison to the altered land that surrounds it. The peregrine falcon, river otter, and greenback cutthroat trout are being reestablished to develop a dynamic ecosystem where plants and animals live as they have for thousands of years.

Yet a national park cannot be an island unto itself. Smog from nearby cities dulls mountain vistas while the threat of acid rain looms like an ominous thunderhead on the horizon. But all is not lost, for our continued care is the key to protection and conservation. The mandate creating Rocky Mountain National Park challenges us to provide for the enjoyment of Rocky's scenic beauty while preserving it for future generations. If we can meet this challenge, our children's children will experience the grandeur of the Rockies much as we have. The majestic mountains, deep canyons, and alpine tundra will continue to inspire generations to come.

J. R. SCHNELZER

A park for all to enjoy lies at the rainbow's end.

Books in The Story Behind the Scenery series: Acadia, Alcatraz Island, Arches, Biscayne, Blue Ridge Parkway, Bryce Canyon, Canyon de Chelly, Canyonlands, Cape Cod, Capitol Reef, Channel Islands, Civil War Parks, Colonial, Crater Lake, Death Valley, Denali, Devils Tower, Dinosaur, Everglades, Fort Clatsop, Gettysburg, Glacier, Glen Canyon-Lake Powell, Grand Canyon, Grand Canyon-North Rim, Grand Teton, Great Basin, Great Smoky Mountains, Haleakala, Hawaii Volcanoes, Independence, Lake Mead-Hoover Dam, Lassen Volcanic, Lincoln Parks, Mammoth Cave, Mesa Verde, Monument Valley, Mount Rainier, Mount Rushmore, Mount St. Helens, National Park Service, National Seashores, North Cascades, Olympic, Petrified Forest, Redwood, Rocky Mountain, Scotty's Castle, Sequoia & Kings Canyon, Shenandoah, Statue of Liberty, Theodore Roosevelt, Virgin Islands, Yellowstone, Yosemite, Zion.

NEW: in pictures—The Continuing Story: Arches & Canyonlands, Bryce Canyon, Death Valley, Everglades, Glacier, Glen Canyon-Lake Powell, Grand Canyon, Hawai'i Volcanoes, Mount Rainier, Mount St. Helens, Olympic, Petrified Forest, Sequoia & Kings Canyon, Yellowstone, Yosemite, Zion.
This *in pictures* series available with translation packages.

Published by KC Publications • Box 94558 • Las Vegas, NV 89193-4558

Inside back cover:
Old-man-of-the-mountain sunflowers
capture the sun's fading light.
Photo by David Muench

Back cover: A bull elk
sports his new rack of velvet antlers.
Photo by Joe Arnold, Jr.

Created, Designed and Published in the U.S.A.
Printed by Dong-A Printing and Publishing, Seoul, Korea
Color Separations by Kedia/Kwangyangsa Co., Ltd.